Pebble®
Plus

LET'S LOOK AT COUNTRIES

# LET'S LOOK AT
# SYRIA

Nikki Bruno Clapper

raintree
a Capstone company — publishers for children

Raintree is an imprint of Capstone Global Library Limited, a company incorporated in England and Wales having its registered office at 264 Banbury Road, Oxford, OX2 7DY – Registered company number: 6695582

**www.raintree.co.uk**
myorders@raintree.co.uk

Edited by Carrie Sheely
Designed by Juliette Peters
Picture research by Tracy Cummins
Production by Laura Manthe
Originated by Capstone Global Library Limited
Printed and bound in India

ISBN 978 1 4747 5309 8 (hardback)
22 21 20 19 18
10 9 8 7 6 5 4 3 2 1

ISBN 978 1 4747 5315 9 (paperback)
22 21 20 19 18
10 9 8 7 6 5 4 3 2 1

**British Library Cataloguing in Publication Data**
A full catalogue record for this book is available from the British Library.

**Acknowledgements**
We would like to thank the following for permission to reproduce photographs: Getty Images: AFP PHOTO/MICHALIS KARAGIANNIS, 14, Diaa Al Din/Anadolu Agency, 17, Ibrahim Ebu Leysi/ Anadolu Agency, 12; iStockphoto: jcarillet, 13, urf, 15; Shutterstock: Anton_Ivanov, 6–7, Cover Top, IKostiuchok, 21, Jakob Fischer, Cover Middle, Cover Back, Kanunnikov Pavel, 22 Top, Leif Stenberg, 1, Martchan, Cover Bottom, 3, Megerya Anna, 9, nale, 4, OBJM, 5, 22–23, 24, Strannik_fox, 10, Tanya Stolyarevskaya, 19, Yerbolat Shadrakhov, 11

# CONTENTS

# Where is Syria?

Syria is a country in Asia. It is part of the Middle East. Syria is more than twice the size of Ireland. Its capital city is Damascus.

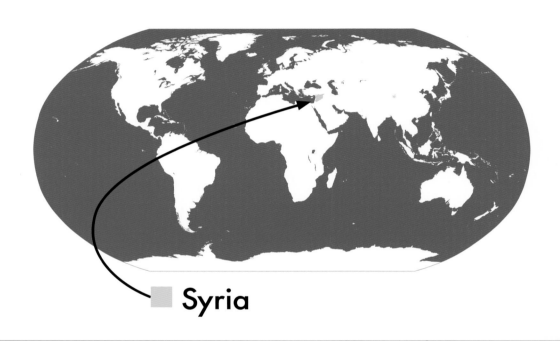

Syria

# A rocky land

Much of Syria is a desert of rock and gravel.

Dust storms cloud the air.

Mountain ranges rise in the west.

Two bodies of water
are important to Syria.
The Mediterranean Sea is on
the west coast. The Euphrates
River flows in the north-east.

# In the wild

Animals roam Syria's desert. Lizards and vipers hide in the rocks. The jerboa jumps around at night. It is a small rodent with long back legs.

lizard

jerboa

# People

Most people in Syria are Arabs. Other groups are Kurds and Armenians. Most Syrians live in the western half of the country.

# At work

Some Syrians farm wheat or cotton for a living. Others help people. They may work in hospitals, schools or restaurants.

# A holy month

Ramadan is a major holiday in Syria. It is a holy month in the Islam religion. People do not eat in the daytime. They feast at night.

Ramadan feast

17

# At the table

Syrians eat a lot of meat, flatbread and salads. One popular meal is kibbeh. Kibbeh are wheat balls filled with lamb or beef.

kibbeh

# A famous site

Broken stone columns rise from the desert. This is the ancient city of Palmyra. It was once a place of great wealth. Today it is in ruins.

# QUICK SYRIA FACTS

Syrian flag

**Name:** Syrian Arab Republic

**Capital:** Damascus

**Other major cities:** Aleppo, Homs, Hama

**Population:** 17,185,170 (July 2016 estimate)

**Size:** 185,180 square kilometres (71,498 sq mi)

**Languages:** Arabic, Kurdish, Armenian

**Money:** Syrian pound

# GLOSSARY

**capital**  city in a country where the government is based

**column**  pillar that supports a building

**gravel**  mixture of sand, pebbles and broken rocks

**Islam**  religion founded in the 600s by Muhammad

**jerboa**  nocturnal jumping rodent of Asia and Africa

**ruins**  remains of a building or other things that have fallen down or been destroyed

**viper**  snake that kills its prey with poison called venom

**wealth**  state of having lots of money

# FIND OUT MORE

## BOOKS

*A Day and Night in the Desert* (Caroline Arnold's Habitats), Caroline Arnold (Picture Window Books, 2015)

*Rashad's Ramadan and Eid al-Fitr* (Holidays and Special Days), Lisa Bullard (Millbrook Press, 2012)

*Syria* (Explore the Countries), Julie Murray (Abdo, 2017)

## WEBSITES

http://thefactfile.org/interesting-facts-syria/
Discover interesting facts about Syria.

http://www.bbc.co.uk/news/world-middle-east-14703856
Learn about key events in Syria's history.

http://www.bbc.co.uk/newsround/23286976
Watch a video about Ramadan, a major holiday in Syria.

# COMPREHENSION QUESTIONS

1. Look at the photo on page 11. How do you think a jerboa's long ears might help it live in the desert?

2. What is a column? What do the columns of Palmyra look like?

3. Name two foods that Syrians eat often.

# INDEX